HOW IT HAPPENED

HAPPENED

PIZZA

The Cool Stories and Facts

Behind Every Slice

H⊙W IT HAPPENED

PIZZA

The Cool Stories and Facts

Behind Every Slice

BY PAIGE TOWLER
ILLUSTRATED BY DAN SIPPLE

union
square
kids

NEW YORK

**union
square
kids**

NEW YORK

ISBN 978-1-4549-4500-0 (hardcover)
ISBN 978-1-4549-4514-7 (paperback)
ISBN 978-1-4549-4501-7 (e-book)

Library of Congress Cataloging-in-Publication Data

Names: Towler, Paige, author. | Sipple, Dan, illustrator.
Title: How it happened: pizza : the cool stories and facts behind every
  slice / by Paige Towler ; Illustrated by Dan Sipple.
Description: New York : Union Square Kids, [2023] | Series: How it happened
  | Includes index. | Summary: "In this nonfiction book filled with
  history, science, facts, and stats, readers can discover how pizza
  became the world's favorite comfort food"-- Provided by publisher.
Identifiers: LCCN 2022061966 (print) | LCCN 2022061967 (ebook) | ISBN
  9781454945000 (hardcover) | ISBN 9781454945147 (trade paperback) | ISBN
  9781454945017 (ebook)
Subjects: LCSH: Pizza--History--Juvenile literature.
Classification: LCC TX770.P58 T68 2023 (print) | LCC TX770.P58 (ebook) |
  DDC 641.82/48--dc23/eng/20230104
LC record available at https://lccn.loc.gov/2022061966
LC ebook record available at https://lccn.loc.gov/2022061967

For information about custom editions, special sales, and premium purchases,
please contact specialsales@unionsquareandco.com.

Printed in Malaysia

Lot #:
2 4 6 8 10 9 7 5 3 1

07/23
unionsquareandco.com

Cover design by Liam Donnelly
Cover art by Becca Clason
Interior illustrations and series logo by Dan Sipple
Interior design by Nicole Lazarus
Created and produced by WonderLab Group, LLC
Photo research by Nicole DiMella
Sensitivity review by Nina Tsang
Copyedited by Susan Hom
Indexed by Connie Binder
Proofread by Molly Reid
Image credits—see page 192

THIS IS DEDICATED TO MY PARENTS, AND TO THE VERY FIRST PEOPLE WHO MADE CHEESE. MY LIFE WOULD NOT BE THE SAME WITHOUT YOU. —P.T.

Table of Contents

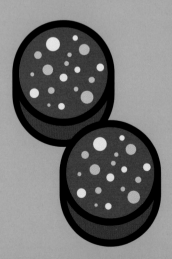

for

Pizza

Pizza, Pizza, Everywhere

Can you imagine a world without pizza? Without all that oozy cheese, sweet and tangy sauce, or crispy crust? Today, you can find almost any kind of pizza, made of almost any ingredient you can think of, and in almost any location.

Pizzas come with tons of different sauces, crust thickness, and toppings. Want a barbecue chicken pizza? No problem. A pizza with no cheese and extra broccoli? You've got it! Gluten-free crust? Take your pick! And that's just in the United States. Travel across the world and you'll find pies that appeal to uniquely different tastes. In fact, you could probably spend the rest of your life trying out new kinds of pizza and still never try them all!

For most people throughout history, life without pizza was the reality. At least, when it came to the pizza you think of today. So what were the very first pizzas like? How did they stack up to the pizza we know today?

Get ready to take a bite out of the history of pizza, from its ancient origins to its official appearance in Italy, and from its journey to the United States to its spread across the globe—and even into space! So what are you waiting for? Dig in!

How It All Started

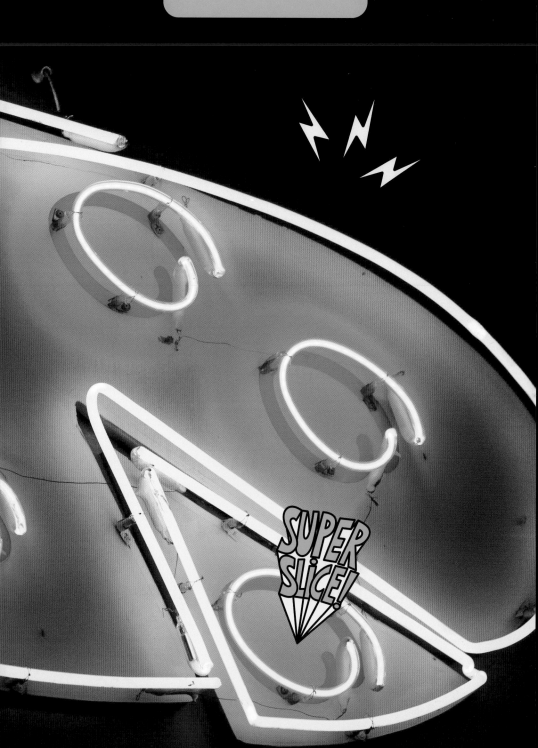

CHAPTER ONE
What's in a Slice?

Delivering the Dough

Today, grabbing a slice of pizza is pretty easy no matter where you are. You can get a whole pie delivered to your home, grab a slice at a local pizzeria, pop a frozen pizza in the oven, or make your own from scratch. But for most of human history, it was a totally different story.

Forget having a whole pizza delivered—it was difficult just to get the ingredients that make up a pie! To understand the origins of ooey-gooey cheese pizza, we need to trace the origins of pizza's most important parts: cheese, tomato sauce, and bread.

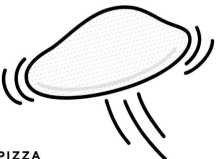

Some of the oldest
known evidence
of bread comes
from 14,000-year-
old breadcrumbs
found at
an ancient
campfire site
in Jordan.

Pizza as we know it isn't exactly new. After all, it's been around for at least two centuries. However, the ingredients weren't always in the forms you might recognize. Some 75,000 years ago, humans in western Asia began eating wild grains known as einkorn and emmer. Over many thousands of years, these cereal grains transformed into some of the varieties that are more common today, such as wheat. Around 14,000 years ago, people began using wheat to make bread. Before then, they often chewed the wheat kernels raw.

For much of prehistoric history, humans were nomadic—meaning they often traveled from place to place in groups or tribes. By 12,000 years ago, however, more and more people were settling down in permanent

Wheat

Chicomecóatl, the Aztec goddess of corn

Gods of Grain

Back before a person could just call up a pizza place for some speedy delivery, humans dedicated much of their lives to farming. Bad crops or harsh winters could cause tough times and even starvation. Because of this, cultures around the world—from the Aztecs in Central America to ancient societies in China to the Māori in New Zealand—often believed in and prayed to gods of agriculture. They believed that these gods could protect crops and create bountiful harvests. For the Romans, this deity was Ceres, the goddess of grain. The English word "cereal" comes from her name.

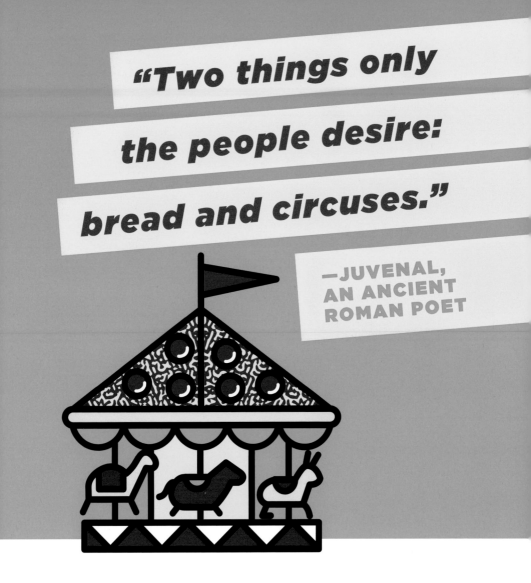

"Two things only the people desire: bread and circuses."

—JUVENAL, AN ANCIENT ROMAN POET

homes and setting up farms. People in the Middle East, where wheat was plentiful, harvested the wheat by separating the edible grains from their long stalks. Then they ground the grain into a fine powder.

They would then mix this powder with water, making a sticky dough that could be baked into . . . bread! Over time, wheat spread across much of Europe, western Asia, and parts of northern Africa. Humans had taken an important first step in creating a culinary masterpiece.

Say Cheese!

Don't reach for a pizza slice just yet! Even though bread was on the scene, cheese had yet to make its appearance. Historians aren't entirely sure when humans first started enjoying cheesy goodness, but it may have been around the time sheep and goats were domesticated, some 11,000 years ago. Today, there are many kinds of cheese made from the milk of animals, like cows, goats, sheep, and even water buffalo. The first cheese was likely made from goat or sheep milk—and it may have been created by accident.

Fun with Fermentation

Fermentation is a controlled and purposeful breaking down of food or liquid. It's a type of rot that you can still eat! For thousands of years, fermentation has been used as a way to preserve foods that might otherwise go bad.

Historians think that ancient humans stored milk in pouches or containers they crafted from sheep stomachs. The stomachs of many animals—including sheep—have a special substance, known as an enzyme, that can cause chemical reactions to occur. In a living animal's stomach, enzymes help digest food. When the stomachs were used as containers, the enzymes that were present would have begun to break down the milk. This process, called **curdling**, causes the milk to transform partly into solid lumps, called curds. While lumpy milk bits may not sound appetizing, they can actually be delicious. That's because those lumps are cheese!

Once humans had discovered cheese, they wanted to make more of it. By around 8,000 years ago, people had set up ways to make cheese on purpose. How did they do it? Much in the same way that cheese is still made today. First, cheesemakers start by pouring milk into huge containers known as vats. Then, they add special kinds of bacteria

Cheddar
cheese was
created
around the
1500s.

and enzymes to the milk. This begins the process of curdling the milk. Over time, the milk separates into curds, and a remaining liquid called whey. Cheesemakers then remove the whey. They heat these salty curds, which lets out even more whey. Now the curds are pressed together, molded into shapes, and left to age.

The earliest cheeses were likely soft or crumbly, with mild to salty and slightly funky flavors—like feta, cottage cheese, or some

A cheesemaker makes mozzarella in a vat.

soft goat cheeses. Over time, people began experimenting and refining the cheesemaking process, creating new methods to make different types of cheese. They added salt or strained the curds and pressed them into blocks. They sometimes let the cheese sit to age and ferment, which would give it a stronger flavor. People like the ancient Romans made many varieties of cheese. Some hard cheeses were even given to Roman soldiers to eat while they were on the go.

Water buffalo

Still, cheese wasn't quite ready for pizza. Today, the most common cheese used on a pizza pie is mozzarella. This is because the cheese is extra creamy and melts evenly and quickly. The first version of mozzarella may have appeared around 2,000 years ago in southern Italy. Back then, it was probably made from sheep's milk—not from the water buffalo milk traditionally used in modern mozzarella. Historians aren't exactly sure when, but water buffalo were eventually introduced to the region, and people started using their milk for cheesemaking. It wasn't until the eighteenth century that water buffalo cheese exploded in popularity. People started breeding more herds, and as a result, mozzarella became a common and popular type of cheese.

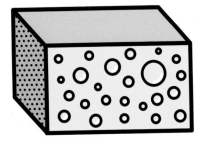

The Secret Sauce

Spaghetti with pomodoro sauce, caprese salad, bruschetta—some of the most iconic Italian dishes feature tomatoes. Surely the tomato comes from Italy, right? Nope! In fact, most people in Europe before the 1500s had never seen or heard of a tomato.

The first tomatoes grew nearly halfway around the world in South America's Andes Mountains. The first tomato fruits were smaller and harder than tomatoes today— almost like berries. Over time, people across South and Central America bred them to be larger and juicier. It wasn't until the sixteenth century that the tomato arrived in Europe, when Spanish explorers brought the fruit back on their ships after traveling to the Americas.

For many European people, the tomato was considered gross, or even dangerous. Back then, lots of wealthy people in Europe

"Knowledge is knowing tomato is a fruit. Wisdom is knowing not to put it in a fruit salad."

—MILES KINGTON, BRITISH JOURNALIST

ate on plates made with a poisonous material called lead. When tomatoes were plopped onto these plates, their acidic juices would cause the poisonous lead to seep into the fruit. As a result, lots of people got sick. And they blamed the tomato!

Luckily, some of the poorer people in Spain and Italy who did not eat on these fancy but dangerous plates began to incorporate the new food into their meals. On top of that, the Italians created pizza's missing ingredient: tomato sauce.

Historians think people who lived in southern Italy first invented the simple (but delicious) sauce by mashing up ripe tomatoes and adding olive oil. Some chefs also added other ingredients, like garlic, basil, and salt. It had taken almost 14,000 years, but now the ingredients to make pizza were finally together in the same place.

The Italian word for tomato, *pomodoro,* means "golden apple." Historians think this may mean that Italians first saw yellow tomatoes.

Tomato Fight!

After their introduction some 500 years ago, tomatoes have become popular in Spain . . . and so has throwing them! Since 1945, in the town of Buñol, tens of thousands of people gather at La Tomatina festival each year to pelt each other with soft, mushy tomatoes. By the end of the friendly food fight, both the people and the town are covered in smashed tomatoes.

CHAPTER TWO
Paving the Way for Pizza

Fantastic Flatbreads

Even though the ingredients for pizza took a long time to come together in one place, that didn't mean that there were no pizzalike foods at all. In fact, people have been making early versions of pizza for at least 6,000 years. One of the oldest written recipes describes a type of Sumerian flatbread made from flour, water, and salt.

Flatbreads are breads that are baked into flat discs or sheets. (Not so shocking, given their name.) Flatbreads are flat because they're often made without an ingredient called

 yeast. Yeast is a tiny organism—a fungus, in fact. When yeast is baked into bread or pastries, it makes them rise and puff up.

Today, pizza doughs are often made with yeast, which makes them light and airy. Flatbreads, on the other hand, are often dense, thick, and chewy. Even so, the Sumerians used these flatbreads as sort of proto-pizza crusts. They sometimes added toppings to these flatbreads, such as chopped onions or leeks, as well as olive oil and herbs. Of course, if you were at a restaurant today and ordered a slice of pizza only to receive a flatbread, you might very well send it back—they're not exactly identical!

Versions of flatbreads were developed all across the world, some more similar to pizza than others. In ancient Egypt, people made flatbreads from wheat and barley. Some recipes for breads were even painted on the walls of tombs! A similar food was eaten in ancient Greece, where some historians think people began to top the breads with sprinkles of soft cheeses.

Feasting Yeast

Yeast is a living fungus that exists in nature all around you: in tree sap, in overripe fruit, and more. Today, you can find yeast sold in small packets at the grocery store, but some bakers grow their own yeast from scratch, too. When yeast is mixed into a dough, all the tiny organisms "eat" the sugars in the wheat flour. As they feast, the solid sugars turn into gassy carbon dioxide, making the dough rise.

What happens to the yeast after it's finished doing its gassy business? A pizza oven is too hot for the yeast to stay alive—but it sticks around as a delicious flavor that you associate with baked dough.

In Morocco, *madfouna* is a traditional flatbread stuffed with meat, onions, and spices, and cut into slices. In ancient India, people topped a flatbread called naan with garlic and herbs or used it to scoop up sauces and other foods. People developed flatbreads with other ingredients, too, such as corn tortillas in Mesoamerica. All of these delicious foods are still eaten today!

Madfouna is traditionally cooked by being buried with hot stones in hot desert sands.

Location Legends

You may have heard that pizza actually comes from China, and not Italy. Is this true? Not exactly. Like in other regions around the world, people in ancient China dined on versions of flatbreads. One of these was *cong you bing*, or scallion pancakes. Made from thin layers of fried dough sprinkled with scallions (an onion-like vegetable), these savory pancakes are still enjoyed today. However, as with other flatbreads, they are pretty different from what we think of as pizza. So where does this myth come from? It might be thanks to the Italian explorer and trader named Marco Polo. In the thirteenth century, Polo traveled to China, where he developed a taste for scallion pancakes. In fact, he loved them so much, he brought the recipe back to Italy.

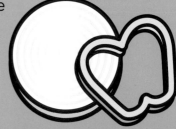

Heating Up

As chefs took the first steps toward creating pizza, people were also perfecting another hidden ingredient behind pizzas: the oven. Human ancestors have been cooking since they discovered how to control fire at least 300,000 years ago. Much of this cooking was done in pits dug into the earth or over and around campfires.

Over thousands of years, humans began creating new ways to cook food. People may have been creating very basic forms of ovens or stone pits as long ago as 30,000 years. By 6,000 years ago, people in parts of Europe and Asia were building aboveground ovens made of clay, stone, or bricks. These ovens were often domed, which trapped the heat inside and allowed people to control cooking temperatures. They also were safer to use indoors than an open fire. To heat the ovens, people burned hay or wood. As cities and populations grew, people created larger ovens that could bake more bread.

For the most part, these closed wood-fired ovens were perfect for making pizzas. The closed oven's heat could soar to high temperatures, allowing the pizza crust to get nice and crispy quickly so that the cheese melted but other toppings didn't burn. Plus, the thick walls of clay, stone, or brick trapped plenty of heat.

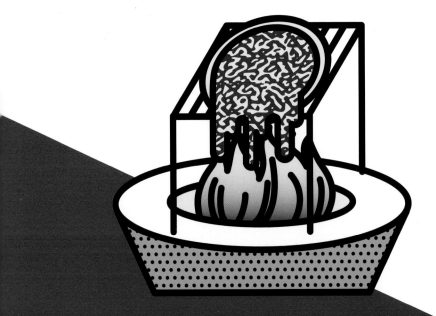

Making Matzah

According to Jewish scripture, the traditional flatbread called matzah (or matzo) was created some 3,000 years ago by the Israelites. They were enslaved in ancient Egypt. When they fled to their sacred promised lands, the Israelites did not have time to add yeast to let their dough rise. Instead, as they traveled, the sun cooked the dough into flat, cracker-like squares, now known as matzah.

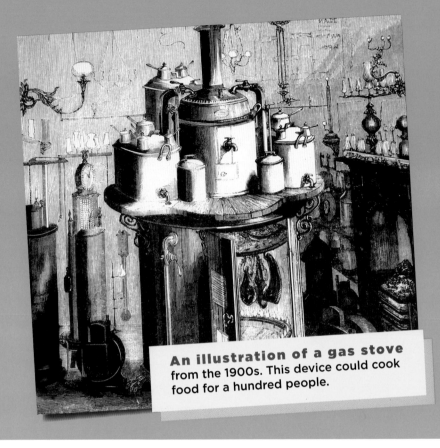

An illustration of a gas stove from the 1900s. This device could cook food for a hundred people.

In 1826, British inventor James Sharp patented an oven design that relied on gas for its fuel. Then, in 1896, American inventor William Hadaway Jr. patented a version that used electricity. Even so, many modern pizzerias use wood-fired pizza ovens similar to the ones used thousands of years ago.

Cooked food often provides more nutrients than raw food. Scientists think that cooked meals caused humans' brains to grow larger over time!

Fanning the Flames

Scientists continue to discover new evidence around the history of human ancestors and the uses of controlled fire for cooking foods. Evidence found in places across Africa, Europe, and Asia suggests that the use of fire was becoming more common around 400,000 years ago. And the very first uses may be even older than that: Archaeologists discovered evidence of fire and firemaking tools in Israel that may be about 800,000 years old. Some experts think that controlled fire may be even older. A researcher in Kenya believes she has found evidence of controlled fire that could be about 1.6 million years old!

"**The blazing fire makes flames and brightness out of everything thrown into it.**"

—MARCUS AURELIUS, ROMAN EMPEROR

CHAPTER THREE
Pizza Is Born

The Source of a Slice

Around the world, people were making flatbreads and cheese. So why is it that one place in particular—Italy—is known as the birthplace of pizza?

In the late fifteenth and early sixteenth centuries, explorers who set sail from Europe set foot on lands they previously didn't know existed. These regions, which included North America and South America, became known in Europe as the New World.

In the 1500s, Spanish explorer Hernán Cortés invaded parts of Central America and the Caribbean. When European explorers arrived in the Americas, they often seized lands for their own countries—even though

those lands were already lived on and owned. Soldiers captured Indigenous peoples across the Americas or wiped them out. Even people who did not intend to colonize, or establish control over the local people and land, could cause harm just by showing up. They brought many diseases with them, including ones that the peoples of the Americas had never encountered before. Entire civilizations fell.

These voyages changed history in Europe and other continents as well. People all over the world began to interact with each other in new ways and learn new ideas. These changes extended to the culinary world, too. When Cortés sailed back to Spain, he brought along many of his "discoveries," including tomatoes. The juicy fruit reached Italy in 1548.

The Italians now had access to tomatoes and, thanks to the wide introduction of water buffalo in the Middle Ages, mozzarella cheese. The truth is, though, historians aren't sure exactly when true pizza was first invented. However, they do think it was sometime in the sixteenth or seventeenth centuries around Naples. While neither mozzarella nor tomatoes were very popular yet, impoverished people living in the area often had to make do with

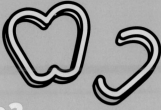

Just like no one knows when the very first pizza was made, historians aren't sure where the name "pizza" comes from. Some think it may come from the ancient Greek word for pastry. Others think it may be from an old Germanic word, *pizzo*, meaning "small bite," or "morsel."

the ingredients they had at hand: dough, tomato sauce, mozzarella, and ovens. And pizza was born!

By the late 1700s, pizza had become somewhat common. Official documents from the time confirm that there were *pizzaioli,* or pizzamakers. A recipe for a pizza made with cheese and tomato sauce appears in a

Modern-day Naples

Anatomy of the Original Pizza

Take a look at what makes up a traditional Neapolitan pizza—meaning a pizza from Naples.

• **The crust is traditionally made** with flour, water, salt, and yeast, and it is baked just until brown spots start to appear around the edges. Neapolitan crust is usually thin with pillowy edges and is soft and slightly chewy.

• **To make the pizza sauce,** chefs often use a special variety of tomato called San Marzano. The sauce is often mixed with olive oil, salt, and garlic, and it can be slightly sweet and acidic thanks to the special tomatoes.

• **On top of the sauce** are small melted pieces of buffalo mozzarella, or mozzarella made from the milk of water buffalo. It is mild and creamy, and normally does not cover the entire pizza.

• **Unlike many modern pizzas,** traditional Neapolitan pizzas are often not cut into slices. Instead, people eat them using a knife and fork.

1799 book, too. But pizza was only eaten among the poor, working-class people in Naples. For them, pizza was perfect—it was cheap, easy to make, and could be eaten quickly or on the go. First sold by street vendors, it soon showed up in shops as people opened places dedicated just to pizza. However, nobles often looked down on pizza as being a food eaten by commoners. Not only were they biased—they were seriously missing out.

"Ideas are like pizza dough: made to be tossed around."

—ANNA QUINDLEN, AUTHOR

Who Was Queen Margherita?

Margherita of Savoy was born in 1851 in Turin, a city in northern Italy. Her father, a duke, died when she was young, but Margherita led a comfortable childhood, with a thorough education that was rare for princesses at the time. When she was sixteen years old, Margherita married Prince Umberto, who was in line to be the future king. (He was also her first cousin.) When Umberto officially became the king of Italy in 1878, Margherita became the queen of Italy.

As queen, Margherita played an important role in making sure the royal family stayed popular throughout the kingdom. She made many donations and befriended artists, who created works that praised the royals. She also toured the kingdom, and legend says it was during one of these tours when she enjoyed a slice of pizza.

Queen Margherita

Fit for a Queen

For over a century, many wealthy people in Naples turned down their noses at pizza. That was until it was given the royal seal of approval by the queen of Italy herself.

In 1889, Queen Margherita and her husband, King Umberto I, decided to pay a visit to Naples. According to legend, Queen Margherita was interested in trying the cuisine of the local common people—which, of course, was pizza. She asked the most famous local pizza place to prepare a few pizzas for her. The chef, a man named Raffaele Esposito, whipped up several different versions. As the story goes, one in particular delighted the queen: a simple pizza featuring tomato sauce, mozzarella, and basil. The colors of the ingredients matched those on Italy's flag. In honor of the queen, Esposito gave this pizza the name it still carries today: the margherita.

As news spread of the queen and the margherita, pizza started to rise in popularity. People wanted to try this fashionable food fit for a queen. In fact, pizza started becoming so popular that pizza shops had soon spread across Italy.

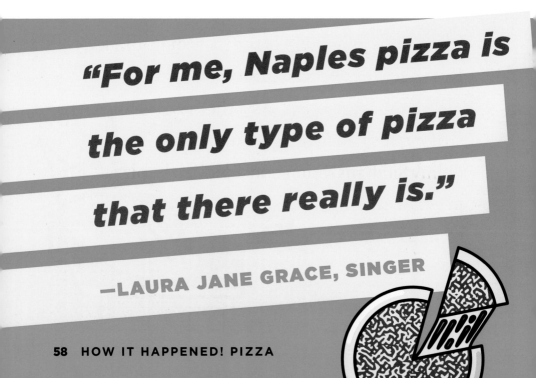

"For me, Naples pizza is the only type of pizza that there really is."

—LAURA JANE GRACE, SINGER

Sfincione

People in different regions were also creating new versions inspired by their own local ingredients. Not far from Naples, on the southern island of Sicily, a different dish had been developing. Known as *sfincione,* this pizzalike food featured a base of thick, moist flatbread called focaccia. It was traditionally covered with vegetables, anchovies, crunchy breadcrumbs, and sometimes grated cheese. Many Sicilians didn't consider it to be pizza— it's just sfincione! However, its popularity proved that cheesy flatbreads had become an iconic Italian food.

The amount
of pizza
eaten in the
United States
in just one day
could cover
more than
75 football
fields.

Tlayuda Talk

Just as pizza uses ingredients that became local to Naples, a flatbread called *tlayuda* uses the unique tastes of Mexico. In this case, the dough is a crispy corn shell, often topped with a mild local cheese called *quesillo*. The tlayuda is then covered with toppings like grilled meats, avocado, salsas, and more.

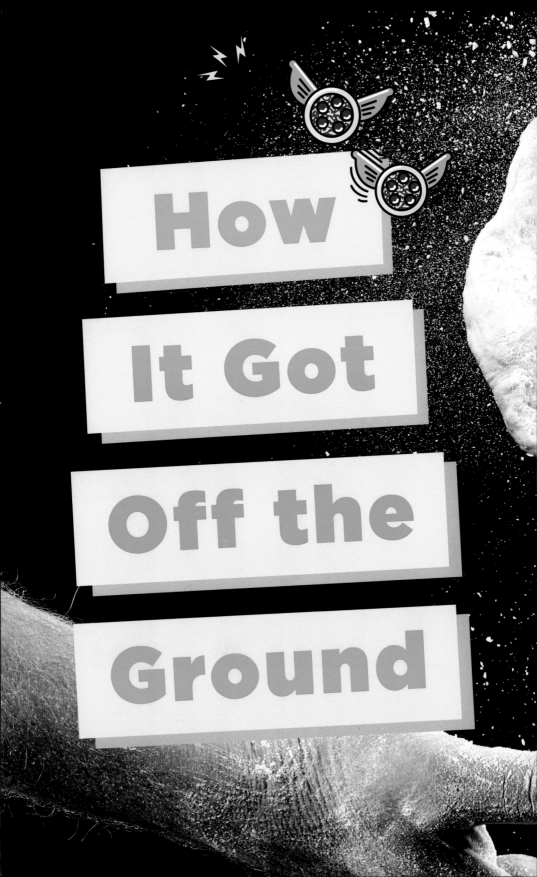

How It Got Off the Ground

CHAPTER FOUR
A Long-Distance Delivery

Hot Pizza, Hard Times

By the end of the nineteenth century, pizza was becoming extremely popular across Italy. But it had yet to make its mark on the rest of the world. So how did it go global?

The first step to sharing the dish came in the late 1800s, as millions of people began to leave, or emigrate, from Italy. Throughout the nineteenth century, the country had been facing difficult times. Although Italy today is a united country, for much of history it was made up of several independent kingdoms. Over the centuries, other countries, kingdoms, and empires had conquered some of these Italian kingdoms to control them. In 1815, a movement began to bring the Italian

kingdoms together under Italian rule. This movement was called the Risorgimento. Italians faced battles for independence against the foreign rulers who had been controlling the different Italian kingdoms. The Italian troops succeeded, and in 1861, the Kingdom of Italy was established.

The wars had left many people poor or homeless, especially in the northern part of the country. People in the south were suffering, too. Many lived in poverty, which became worse during a series of natural disasters. Near Naples, the volcano Mount Vesuvius erupted several times over the nineteenth century. Then, in 1908, a powerful earthquake struck the region and caused a tsunami. Facing even tougher times in an already devastated area, many people chose to leave the country to seek better lives or even just find temporary work elsewhere. Wherever they went, they brought their cultures and customs with them . . . including their recipes for pizza.

The ruins of Pompeii as it looks today.

A Piece o' Pompeii

In the sixteenth century, an architect named Domenico Fontana was looking to construct a well in a field near Naples. Instead, as he dug, he discovered something else: an entire hidden city! Fontana had stumbled upon the ruins of Pompeii, an ancient Roman city that was completely buried by the eruption of Mount Vesuvius in the year 79. Because the city had been buried by ash, it remains almost perfectly preserved, despite being more than 1,500 years old. Among the ruins are many intact ovens, which were used to bake pizzalike flatbreads and other foods. In fact, the ovens are nearly identical to pizza ovens still used today.

New Places, New Pizzas

Some Italian immigrants remained somewhat close to home by moving to other European countries. However, many people chose to try their luck in the Americas. At the time, several countries in North and South America were becoming known not only for their opportunities, but also for their relatively open policies toward immigrants. As Italian people began to settle in these places, they brought along their own cultures as well as adapted to new ones. When they cooked Italian foods, they began to use the new ingredients their new homes offered. Over time, this led to the creation of unique and new kinds of pizzas.

Starting in the mid-1800s, some two million Italians immigrated to Argentina. The country was experiencing economic growth, which appealed to immigrants.

Cassoulet

General Tso's chicken

Trade Ya!

Pizza is not the only dish that has been adapted by multiple cultures. Many foods around the world were created as a result of immigration or trade between countries. Check out some culinary creations that exist thanks to the interactions of multiple cultures.

• **Cassoulet:** *Cassoulet* is a traditional French stew made by simmering beans and other ingredients. Yet for much of history, cassoulet was impossible for French people to make—that's because beans originally come from Central and South America. They didn't arrive in Europe until the sixteenth century.

• **General Tso's Chicken:** Created by Chinese American chef Tsung Ting Wang, General Tso's chicken was inspired by a recipe originally created by Chinese chef Peng Chang-kuei. However, to suit American tastes, Wang added a crispier breading and a lot more sugar.

• **Omurice:** This beloved Japanese dish— featuring a fluffy egg omelet draped over Japanese fried rice and topped with ketchup—was created in the early 1900s and was inspired by French omelets.

Omurice

It also had climates somewhat similar to those around Italy, and many people in the country shared the same religion: Roman Catholicism. For these reasons and more, Italian immigrants began to pour in—including many people from Genoa, a region in northern Italy that had been affected by the battle for independence and unification.

The most famed foods in Genoa were slightly different from those in Naples. In

Genoa, people ate a dense, rich flatbread known as focaccia, often topped with herbs and onions. Of course, as pizza became popular across Italy, the Genoese people soon adopted that dish, too, tweaking it to match their own preferences.

As it happened, one of the Genoese people who left for Argentina was a baker. There, he came up with a brand-new kind of pizza especially suited to fit both local and Genoese tastes. Known as the *fugazza,* this pizza featured a thick, focaccia-like crust and was topped with tons of onions and cheese. It became a hit: People in Argentina still dine on fugazza today, and

Fugazza comes from the Genoese word for focaccia, *fugassa.* *Focaccia* was the ancient Roman name for bread baked under coals.

the dish has even spread to other countries and continents.

In each place they immigrated, Italians created new versions of pizzas influenced by local ingredients and preferences. In Brazil, where more than one million Italians immigrated, they developed what became known as the *pizza à portuguesa*. This pizza had some pizza "classics," like sausage, ham, mozzarella, and tomato, but it also contained many new additions: bell peppers, boiled eggs, and sometimes even green peas or corn. Pizza was on the rise across South America . . . and would be all the more so on another continent to the north.

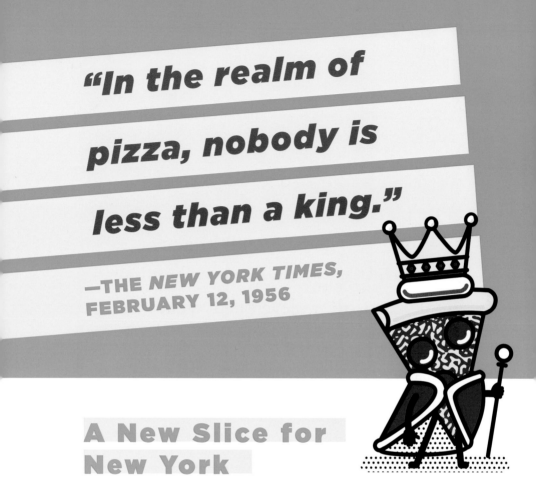

> **"In the realm of pizza, nobody is less than a king."**
>
> —THE *NEW YORK TIMES*, FEBRUARY 12, 1956

A New Slice for New York

One of the most famous versions of pizza around the world is the American style. Back in the 1800s, the largest number of Italian immigrants headed for the United States. By 1920, some four million Italians had moved to the country. In 1905, Italian immigrant Gennaro Lombardi opened one of the first ever pizza restaurants in the

United States. Located in New York City, it was called Lombardi's. Soon, more pizza places followed, mostly located in Italian American neighborhoods.

As in other places, the pizzas crafted in New York evolved to include local ingredients and to appeal to American tastes. Instead of being blended from fresh San Marzano tomatoes, their tomato sauce was largely made from canned tomatoes—and sweetened to account for the average American's love of sugar.

The cheese was different, too. Unlike Italian mozzarella, which was made from the milk of water buffalo and formed into soft balls, American mozzarella came from cows' milk and was formed into firm blocks, which were then grated. (A lot more cheese made it onto the pizza, too!)

New York City in the early 1900s

And, of course, New York pizzas had one more important difference: the crusts. Thanks to the availability of certain flours— and, according to legend, the minerals in New York City tap water—these crusts were thin, hard, and crunchy.

Though pizzas were made with local ingredients, they failed to take off in popularity. Relations between long-settled Americans and newly arrived immigrants were often strained. In the late 1800s and early 1900s, millions of immigrants arrived in the United States, searching for job opportunities, safety, and more. They came from many different countries, and usually settled in cities where work could be found. This often caused overcrowding in already crowded places. Tensions between Americans and immigrants flared. Many Americans inaccurately blamed new immigrants for the nation's economic, social, and criminal problems. Because of this, immigrants often faced violence, segregation, and many other dangerous conditions.

These prejudices also extended to the foods eaten by immigrants. Many Americans viewed pizza as strange and foreign. Pizza had officially landed in the United States, but it had yet to take over.

A Helping of Herbs

Many people love to sprinkle Parmesan, red pepper flakes, or oregano onto their pizza slices. Today, oregano is one of the most popular seasonings in the United States. From soups to meatballs to pastas, and even ice cream, dried oregano adds an earthy, sharp taste. In fact, Americans eat more than fourteen million pounds of oregano every year. But until the 1940s, very few Americans had even heard of it. A member of the mint family, the oregano plant is native to the Mediterranean and parts of western Asia. And that's mostly where it remained, until American soldiers gave the herb a try while they were stationed in Italy during World War II. The soldiers weren't done eating oregano once they headed back home—so they brought it with them!

Oregano

A Nation of Pizza

As the 1930s drew to a close, most people around the world had other things on their mind besides pizza. Adolf Hitler, the political leader of the German Nazi Party, had become a dictator, meaning a ruler with total power. In 1939, Hitler began invading other countries, setting in motion what would become known as World War II.

World War II was a devastating time for people around the world. After the war ended in 1945, many people were eager to turn toward the future and think about something other than fighting. During this time, pizza became a rising star in the United States. In fact, Italian culture in general was on the rise across the country in the 1950s.

Dean Martin (left) and **Frank Sinatra** (right)

Legendary singer and actor Frank Sinatra—still considered an Old Hollywood icon today—was an Italian American. Dean Martin, another Italian American singer and actor, referenced a "big pizza pie" in one of his hit love songs, "That's Amore." And although it didn't include pizza, the 1955 version of the Disney movie *Lady and the Tramp* featured Italian food when the two canine main characters dine on a bowl of spaghetti.

Pizza was quickly becoming an American icon. According to a newspaper article from 1956, it was even on its way to replace the hot dog as the country's favorite fast food. The dish started showing up at state fairs and drive-in movie theaters, where moviegoers could watch films on giant screens from their cars while they snacked on a slice.

Why a Pie?

You've probably heard pizza referred to as a pizza pie. But let's be real, it's definitely not the kind of sweet pie you eat for dessert! So where did this term come from? People aren't completely sure, but the name may have been created by early pizza vendors trying to make the dish seem more familiar to Americans in the early 1900s. To drum up business, they described the dish as an Italian pie. Or it may have simply been because a pizza has some of the same components as a pie does—dough and filling. Either way, the name stuck.

Deep-dish pizza

All the while, pizza developed and continued to morph into new styles across the nation. Some of these pizza versions changed up the bread, some changed up the toppings—one even changed up the order of a pizza's layers!

While Chicago had a large Italian American community, two chefs decided that they wanted to take things a step further and try something different: In 1943, they opened a restaurant featuring a dish that was almost more pie than pizza pie.

One popular
food in Rhode
Island is pizza
strips: pizza
dough covered
in tomato sauce
and cut into
thin slices.

Known as a deep-dish pizza, this version features a thick dough that bakes in a pie-like dish, creating a crust that folds up around the edges. A large amount of cheese is then put onto the crust, followed by any toppings—such as bell peppers or sausage. Finally, a layer of chunky tomato sauce is poured on top. The whole pie is cooked until it is bubbling hot, and then served by cutting it into slices. While the dish only somewhat resembles its Neapolitan origins, it has become an iconic Chicagoan food.

"Pineapple on pizza is MY JAM— with ham."

—DWAYNE "THE ROCK" JOHNSON, ACTOR

Hawaiian Pie?

In the United States, one of the most divisive pizza toppings is probably pineapple—people either love it or hate it! This flavorful fruit became popular as a pizza topping with the invention of the Hawaiian pizza, which is topped with pizza and ham. And that's not just any ham—it's a special type known as Canadian bacon. But hang on, because despite the name, this pizza style wasn't invented in Hawaii. That's right—Hawaiian pizza was first invented in Canada in 1962. It was created by a Greek Canadian named Sam Panopoulos, who wanted to spice up his restaurant's menu.

Made in Missouri, St. Louis-style pizza features a superthin crust made without yeast.

And Chicago wasn't the only city slinging pies. In Detroit, Michigan, hungry Americans also began seeking out pizza. In 1946, a restaurant owner named Gus Guerra decided to add pizza to his menu. He started with a recipe not for pizza, but for sfincione that his wife had borrowed from her Sicilian mother. According to legend, Gus didn't have access to the traditional square pans needed to bake sfincione. Instead, he borrowed pans (normally used to store spare car parts) from a local car factory.

Despite what the traditional Sicilian recipe called for, Gus topped his new creation with plenty of cheese and sauce to match the popular pizzas springing up across the country. Over time, this new style of pizza came to be called Detroit pizza.

The innovations didn't stop there. Through the years, pizza recipes continued to take on the flavors and ingredients that were popular in different states. In the 1980s, California chefs began topping pizzas with ingredients that might have seemed unfamiliar elsewhere but were ultra popular within the state. Soon, there were pizzas featuring pesto sauce, barbecue chicken and red onion, avocado, arugula, and even salmon. Pizza had come to represent not just Italy, but the United States— and what's more, there were now pizzas to represent different parts of the country!

Pizza acrobatics is a competition during which professional pizzamakers face off with special dough throwing routines. Competitors twirl, juggle, and throw pizza dough in unique and creative ways.

Anatomy of a Modern Pizza

Today, you can still order yourself an authentic Neapolitan pizza in many parts of the world. But you can also find countless varieties of pizza—some of which are super different than the pizza of 150 years ago!

• **Crust:** Thick, thin, deep-dish, filled with cheese—this is just the start. You can also find pizzas made with vegetable crust, bagel crusts, or crusts that are formed into pockets.

• **Sauce:** While many of the most common pizzas feature tomato sauce, many more are slathered with barbecue sauce, cream sauce, pesto, mayo—or even no sauce at all.

• **Cheese:** Today, pizza chefs around the world experiment with hundreds of different kinds and combinations of cheese, from cheddar to ricotta and everything in between!

• **Toppings:** From caviar in Russia to boiled eggs in Brazil to reindeer in Finland, the sky's the limit on ingredients you want on the top of your pie.

CHAPTER FIVE
Pizza on the Rise

A Meal for the Whole Family

While chefs all over the United States were inventing new types of pizza, change was also afoot in the American home. After World War II, many people moved to a new type of neighborhood, called the **suburbs**. Today, suburbs—which are areas or communities set on the outskirts of busy city centers—are very common. But in the 1950s, they were still a new concept. For people hoping to own houses, the suburbs were very appealing. In fact, after the war, the country experienced major growth in populations in suburbs, home ownership, and the number of children being born.

Whether in the suburbs or in cities, pizza was the perfect way to feed growing families. A large pie could feed several people and could even be customized to include everyone's favorite toppings. Plus, it was ready quickly, saving time spent cooking or doing the dishes. Some home cooks began to write in to food magazines, asking for pizza recipes (of course, home chefs in Italy had known just what to do for many decades, by this point). Stores and companies even began to sell pizza dough mixes, making the whole thing easier and faster.

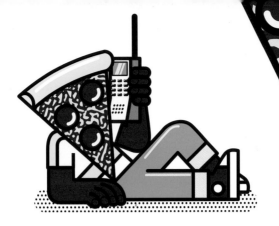

Of course, the easiest and fastest way to get a pizza was often to get one from a pizzeria. However, the suburbs were much more spread out than the city. People relied more on cars, bicycles, and other forms of transportation. This led to another new development for pizza: delivery. Now, busy families could simply call in an order to a pizza place and have it brought directly to their home! With this new convenience, the demand for pizza just kept growing.

Super Chill

Pizza was really starting to heat up, but it had another territory to conquer: the freezer. During the 1950s, higher incomes

Throw That Dough!

At home, people tend to use their hands to spread pizza dough onto a pizza pan, or maybe even use a rolling pin. But if you've ever seen a professional pizzamaker cook a pizza from scratch, then you've probably seen them tossing the dough. A skilled pizzamaker often kneads, or firmly mixes, the pizza dough with their hands before spreading it out into a small circle. They then gently toss the disc into the air, allowing it to spin and stretch. Seems cool, but is it just for show? Nope! Stretching pizza dough with your fingers can cause tears or holes in the disc. By throwing it, the dough stretches evenly and without tearing. Can anyone learn to toss a pizza—and even do it at home? Sure! The key is to spin the dough with your dominant hand, and to catch the dough on its edges instead of the center. Just make sure you have adult supervision when practicing . . . and a space that can get messy!

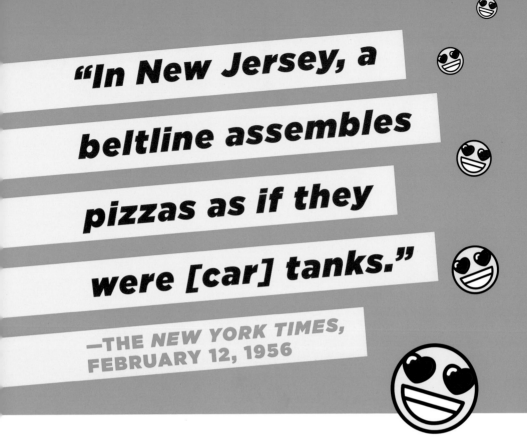

"In New Jersey, a beltline assembles pizzas as if they were [car] tanks."

—THE *NEW YORK TIMES*, FEBRUARY 12, 1956

for families meant more people could afford to buy freezers. This sparked a huge wave in the creation of frozen foods, ready-made meals that could be bought frozen at grocery stores and cooked or heated up at home. The first frozen pizzas appeared around 1950 and hit supermarket shelves by 1954.

By the 1960s, several businesses were hoping to up the frozen pizza game. In 1962, one couple began using a factory to mass-produce frozen pizzas. Their company was called Totino's and quickly became a smash hit. Soon, Totino's expanded to sell other things, such as individual pizza slices and new flavors.

Totino's wasn't the only family business. In 1966, two Wisconsin brothers created Tombstone Pizza. And in 1969, the Quaker Oats Company took over a local frozen pizza company, Mama Celeste, and turned it into a thriving business.

Over time, companies came up with new ways to make their frozen pizzas easier

Before freezers became common in the United States, many people relied on **iceboxes:** containers lined with metal that stayed cold when holding a giant block of ice. Every time the ice melted, it needed to be replaced to keep the contents chilled.

to cook or taste better. Some companies made pizzas that could be cooked in the microwave. In 1995, the Kraft company took things a step further when it created the DiGiorno frozen pizza brand. Unlike other versions, this frozen pizza had crust that would rise to supposedly become soft and pillowy as it baked. Regardless of what brand people used, many were quick to toss a frozen pizza in their shopping cart.

In one American reality show, *Best in Dough,* contestants compete to be the best pizzamakers for a cash prize.

A *Best in Dough* contestant preps his pizza for a school lunch–themed challenge.

Pie!

Leftover Debate

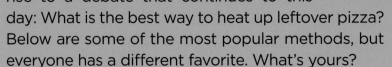

The microwave, which was invented in 1945, created new ways for people to heat up foods. It also helped give rise to a debate that continues to this day: What is the best way to heat up leftover pizza? Below are some of the most popular methods, but everyone has a different favorite. What's yours?

• **Microwave Munching:** Some people claim that the easiest, fastest, and best way to heat cold pizza is by popping it in the microwave. However, there's a trick to it: To avoid letting the pizza get soggy, some people place a microwave-safe mug of water in the microwave as well. This absorbs some of the heat, letting the cheese melt more evenly as the crust slowly warms.

• **Only the Oven:** Lots of people swear that the only "good" way to reheat leftover pizza is by tossing it back in the oven. It may take a bit longer, but the oven can get the cheese back to being nice and gooey.

• **Staying on Top:** Others claim that the best way to reheat pizza is not in the oven, but on it. Reheating leftover pie in a skillet on the stovetop not only lets the cheese melt evenly, but it gets the crust nice and crispy.

• **Keep It Cool:** For some people, the best way to eat leftover pizza is not to warm it up at all! Experts say this is because letting a pizza sit and cool allows its flavors to blend together for one punchy taste.

The rise of fast food allowed people to order from their cars.

Fast-Food Frenzy

In the 1950s, suburbs and freezers weren't the only things booming: Fast-food chains were also on the rise across the nation. The first fast-food chain, White Castle, opened in Kansas in 1921, and different chains across the country were becoming more and more popular.

The rise of fast food was partly thanks to the country's increased use of cars. After the war, the economy was doing very well. More people could afford automobiles—they needed them, too! With spread-out

suburbs and more highways and freeways, people had to rely on cars to get from one place to another. This made fast food super convenient, as people could stop for a quick bite or roll up to the drive-through windows in their cars.

In 1958, two brothers from Kansas decided to bring together two of these growing trends by opening the country's first fast-food pizza chain: Pizza Hut. The next year, a couple in Michigan opened the second, called Little Caesars. Domino's—originally called DomiNick's—opened in Michigan in 1960.

Because these chains needed to make many pizzas—and quickly—they came up with ways to save money and work fast. They often used frozen dough, canned tomatoes, and pre-shredded cheese. This allowed them to expand, growing into multiple locations that spread across the country. It also changed the face of pizza itself! Now, the "standard" of pizza in the United States was becoming something quite different from the Neapolitan pizzas originally brought by immigrants.

Tough Competition

As lots of fast-food places and frozen pizza companies appeared on the scene, businesses were forced to compete with one another for customers. They tried setting themselves apart with slogans, interesting ads, or fun "extras."

Fast-food companies also began to introduce mascots for their brands. Some of the first—like Ronald McDonald or the Burger King—came out in the 1950s and 1960s. Soon, pizza companies got in on

A Canada-based Pizza Hut once sold pizza-scented perfume.

Eau de Slice

the mascot game. In 1962, Little Caesars debuted the Little Caesar character, a toga-wearing mascot who eventually became known for chanting "Pizza! Pizza!" Pizza Hut responded a year later with Pizza Pete, a cartoon version of an Italian chef. In the 1980s, Domino's added its own mascot: the Noid, a pizza villain always defeated by fast delivery.

As time went on, competition between Domino's and Pizza Hut grew especially fierce. An unofficial rivalry developed. Now, each brand needed to do even more to stand out. Pizza Hut ramped up its efforts in the 1980s by creating reading rewards programs. When kids read a certain amount of books, they'd receive a coupon for a free pizza. Then, in 1989, Pizza Hut stepped up its game by offering sponsorships to films, stadiums, and more.

This meant that in exchange for funding from Pizza Hut, a business partner might feature the company in its movie or display the Pizza Hut logo on a giant sports stadium.

Not to be outdone, Domino's also continued to come up with creative ways to get attention. In 2009, the company completely changed its recipes. It launched an enormous ad campaign to spark interest for the recipes—and it worked. Today, both companies continue to innovate to attract customers and avoid being left behind. For example, in 2016, Pizza Hut changed many of its buildings to look much more sleek and modern, while Domino's developed a strong social media presence.

What Hut?

In 1969, Pizza Hut's owners wanted a way to set their company apart from the crowd. They decided to do this by giving their restaurants a unique design: a bright red roof shaped somewhat like a wide-brimmed hat. This made Pizza Hut buildings instantly recognizable. In fact, the design became so iconic that it was even included in the logo.

Over time, however, Pizza Hut began designing more modern-looking buildings instead. So what happens to a Pizza Hut building when it's no longer a Pizza Hut? Well, it often gets bought by another company. This means you might find a veterinarian, a bank, a church, or even a Domino's inside a former Pizza Hut hut!

However, while the rivalry remained unofficial for the two pizza parlor chains, the media—and fans!—took things to the next level. In the 1990s, national newspapers began running features pitting the pizzas of each chain against each other. Newspaper writers and editors would try different slices and then declare a winner. As the Internet became commonplace, things only escalated. Fans devoted blogs and YouTube  videos to rating pies— and only one chain could be crowned pizza king.

Things really came to a head in the era of social media when big-time fans began showing

off tattoos inspired by the two chains. In response, a Domino's in Russia began offering free pizza for a hundred years to anyone who had a Domino's logo tattoo! However, the company underestimated how many people were willing to get tattoos in exchange for a lifetime of pizza, and quickly had to end the promotion. As for Pizza Hut, it wasn't about to be left in the dust. In 2022, the chain partnered with a famous tattoo artist to set up a temporary pizza-themed tattoo parlor. What's more, in the United Kingdom, it began offering limited editions of temporary tattoos that could be scanned with a smartphone and used to . . . order Pizza Hut.

Today, both companies continue to change up their food, logos, and mascots, and the rivalry continues! All of this advertising helped pizza companies—

from fast-food restaurants to frozen pizza brands—spread almost everywhere in the United States. In fact, this marketing made fast-food pizza so popular that it wouldn't just stop there.

"This summer was a [pizza] promotion battleground."

—GERRY DURRELL, EDITOR OF *PIZZA TODAY* MAGAZINE, 1993

In New York City in the 1950s, one slice of pizza cost around 15 cents.

Pepperoni, Please!

Today, pepperoni is the hands-down most popular pizza topping in the United States. These meaty morsels first began appearing in the United States in the early 1900s when Italian immigrants created a new version of dried sausage. Because of the peppers and spices used to flavor the meat, they called it pepperoni, after the Italian word *peperoncino*, which means "little pepper." However, pepperoni remained relatively unknown on a widespread scale until it became popular with fast-food pizza chains in the 1950s. Pepperoni was easy to store and cheap to buy and make, so it was soon gracing fast-food menus across the nation—and it still does today.

TOTALLY! PEPPERONI!

One chef broke a world record for having the most types of cheese on a single pizza: 254.

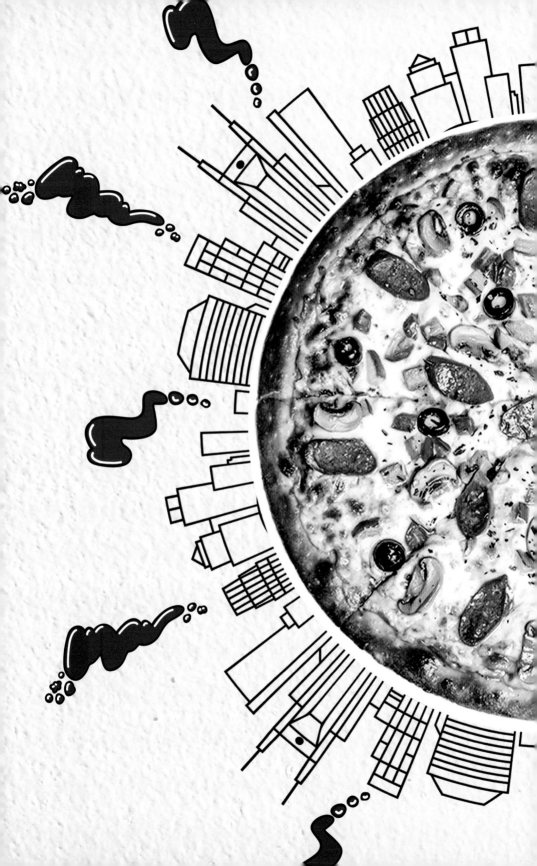

How It Took Over the World

CHAPTER SIX

Pizza in New (and Old) Places

Pass the Pizza

In the history of food, Neapolitan pizza is fairly new—and American pizzas even newer. But pizzalike dishes have existed all over the world for thousands of years. This includes the flatbreads of the ancient world mentioned earlier, and several modern dishes that have evolved from these flatbreads.

Lahmacun

Take, for example, the *lahmacun* (also spelled *lahmajun*). Thought to have originated in Armenia in the Middle Ages, lahmacun features a thin, round flatbread covered in spiced meats and tomato paste. Over time, the dish became popular across parts of western Asia. In addition to the lahmacun, people in Turkey also dine on *pide*, oval-shaped flatbreads folded up and filled with meats, melted cheeses, or both. Some distance away, in 1970s Poland, street vendors looking to create a cheap snack came up with the *zapiekanka*: an open-faced sandwich smothered in meats, vegetables, and sauces.

But also during the twentieth century, something else interesting started to happen: American-style pizzas also began to spread around the globe. In 1968, a Pizza Hut opened in Canada, followed by locations

in Europe and Australia. Domino's went international in 1983, and pizza **franchises** continued to open around the world.

So did the American fast-food pizzas replace other pizzalike foods like pide? Not necessarily! Many pizzalike dishes were different from each other and were viewed as different things—with room for both, depending on your mood. Even though it didn't replace local dishes, American-style pizza became super popular abroad.

Today, Pizza Hut has more than 18,000 restaurants in over 100 countries.

Is It a Sandwich?

Quick question: Is pizza a sandwich? Some people think so! After all, a pizza is sort of a slice of bread with filling on it, like an open-faced sandwich. Thanks to several online discussions and articles that became popular in the 2010s, Internet aficionados began to debate what exactly made a sandwich, and whether certain foods—like pizza, hot dogs, or tacos—qualified as one. For some people, it even became a heated dispute!

Pizza Preferences

As American fast-food pizza popped up across the globe, it started to gain popularity. This happened for a few reasons. The first is called globalization. This is the process of the world becoming more interconnected thanks to things like trade and travel. In the twentieth century, globalization was on the rise thanks to technologies like television, telephones, the Internet, and more.

Toward the end of the twentieth century, the United States became a leader in globalization. This meant that much of American culture was shared with people in other countries, including pizza ads, movies depicting pizza, songs mentioning pizza, and more. Because of this exposure, the concept of American pizza became familiar to people around the world. In some places, like Japan in the 1960s, companies even began to **import**, or bring in, American frozen pizzas so people could try the dish.

A fast-food company in India once offered a "burger pizza": a burger with buns made from pizza dough and filled with cheese and toppings.

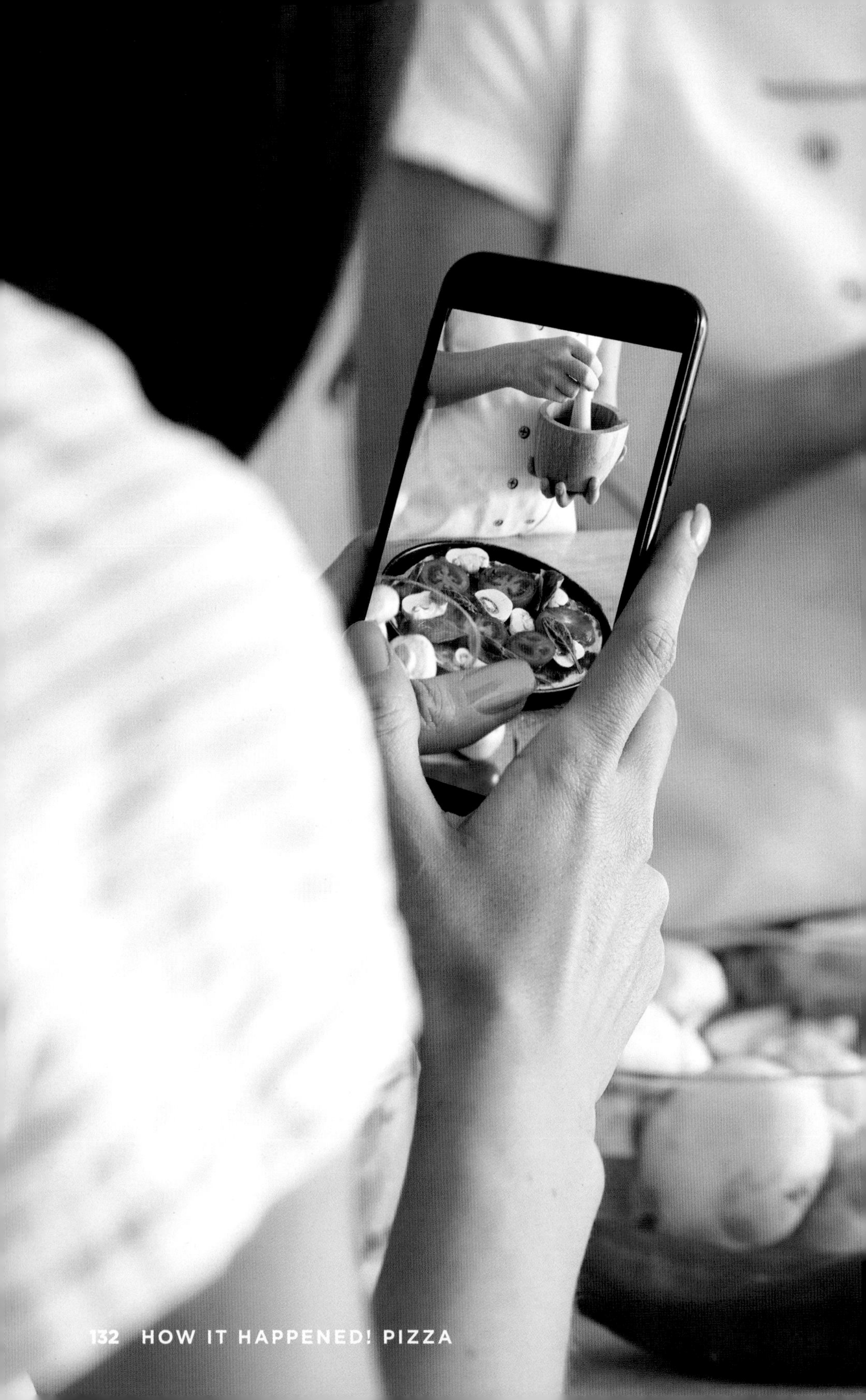

Picture Perfect Pizza

Have you ever marveled at a perfect glistening pizza in an advertisement or commercial? Why do these slices look so extra delicious? It's because there are professionals—called food stylists—who work really hard to make the pie look yummy on camera. This can include using a brush to carefully paint on sauce, using a torch to create a crisp crust, or spraying cooking spray to make those toppings really shine. And when it comes to those toppings, most companies choose to showcase pepperoni, since people associate it most with pizza. In fact, that's the same reason that the pizza emoji features pepperoni, too.

In Japan, Pizza Hut offers pizzas with crusts made from rice dough.

Companies also worked with the same tools they used in the United States to make pizza popular abroad: marketing! As fast-food chains spread, the people running them studied the cultures and trends of other countries. Then, they changed up their menus to appeal to local tastes and wants in different places, in a process called glocalization.

In Japan, for example, Domino's added tuna as a pizza topping. Pizza Hut, meanwhile, offered a pizza with teriyaki sauce (a sweet-and-salty condiment) and mayo. To further meet local tastes, fast-food pizza places also began to sell other menu items not available in the United States, like fish egg pasta.

Fast-food pizza places appealed to lots of people around the world because—just like in the United States—it was cheap, quick, and easy to get. By the 1980s, pizza delivery had become so popular in Japan that people began opening their own pizza delivery restaurants. In fact, across the world, restaurants adapted delivery methods to suit their customers' needs and their city layouts. In many places, delivery people sped across town on scooters or bicycles instead of in cars to wind through heavy traffic. Some companies designed insulated totes or square-shaped bags that could hold pizzas without spilling them, while still keeping them nice and toasty. Now pizza was becoming available across the world in all different styles and flavors.

Strange or Delicious?

Over the years, companies have offered a lot of different attention-getting pizzas. Take a look at some of the most creative and unusual flavors below. Would you try any?

• **How Have You Bean?:** As part of a promotion in the 1990s, one company in the United Kingdom offered a pizza topped with baked beans smothered in cheese.

• **Salty Slice:** In Australia and New Zealand, various companies created a pizza topped with Marmite—a local condiment made from yeast and known for its saltiness.

• **Cone Craving:** In the Middle East, various Pizza Huts began offering pizzas with cone crusts: The crusts were formed into several tiny cones, and then filled with dipping sauce.

Crackers topped with Marmite

There is a pizza restaurant located in Antarctica.

CHAPTER SEVEN

A Slice of Culture

A Pizza for Every Occasion

By the late twentieth century, American-style pizzas dominated the United States as one of the favored cuisines. Different styles from Neapolitan to American had even spread out across the globe, where they quickly transformed into something new. But it didn't stop there. In addition to its global popularity, pizza became a part of everyday culture in many places. This was especially true in the United States, where pizza became not just a dinner or lunch food, but something that could

Aspiring pizzamakers can go to certain culinary schools that specialize in pizza making.

be eaten at school, during parties, on fancy occasions, and even for breakfast!

In 1946, U.S. president Harry Truman enacted the National School Lunch Act. This guaranteed free or cheap lunches for children at public and nonprofit schools across the nation. Soon, many school cafeterias were serving up hot pizza. It was easy to make and could feed a lot of kids. Plus, most kids liked pizza! School pizza lunches also appeared in other countries, such as the United Kingdom and Australia. Some food companies even joined in on the trend. In 1996, the American company Lunchables created ready-to-eat lunch packs that let kids assemble their own mini pizzas. This showed that pizza was becoming an even more common part of the culture in the United States.

WHAT DO YOU THINK?

Is it true that pizza dominates school lunch menus? Take a look at your school's menu (if it has one) or ask your friends and family to look at theirs. How many times a week does the school serve pizza for lunch? Next, try asking a parent or caregiver about their school lunches growing up. How often do they remember eating pizza?

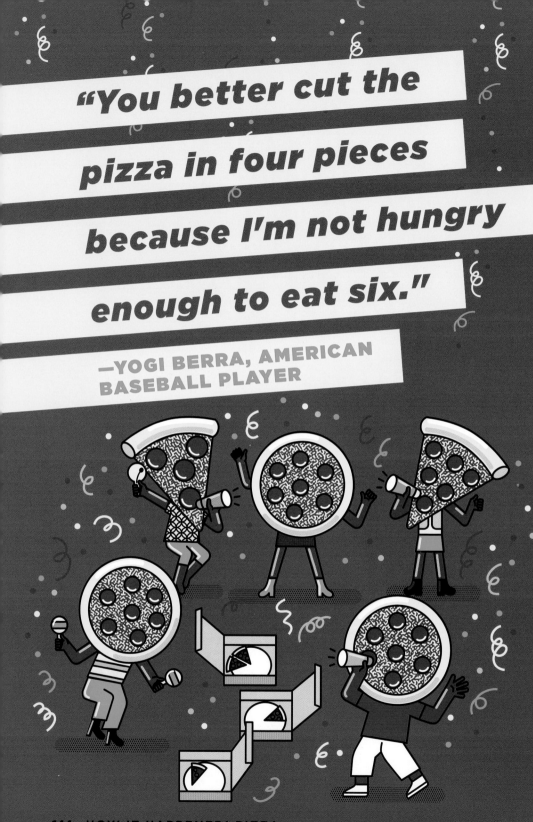

"You better cut the pizza in four pieces because I'm not hungry enough to eat six."

—YOGI BERRA, AMERICAN BASEBALL PLAYER

PIZZA PARTY!

Pizza made its way into new and old American traditions. Since pizza became popular, people have been throwing pizza parties—social events such as slumber parties or birthdays where pizza is served as the main meal. Other people also began to dine on the cheesy discs for fancy occasions, too. Rather than eating pizza from pizza parlors or fast-food places, many people sought out pizzerias and fine-dining Italian restaurants with old-school cooking methods like wood-fired ovens. "Fancy" pizza places often used traditional cooking techniques and prided themselves on fresh ingredients. Some restaurants even topped their pizzas with rare ingredients—like

expensive mushrooms called truffles or even edible gold—that cost much more than the average slice.

In fact, pizza had become so ingrained in American culture that people began to eat it all day long. For breakfast, some people ate Bagel Bites: half bagels topped with sauce, cheese, and toppings. For lunch, others might nosh on Pizza Pockets, hot pockets of pastry stuffed with pizza sauce and toppings that could be heated in the microwave. And don't forget the snacks!

One restaurant sells a pizza that is covered in caviar—and costs more than $12,000 U.S. dollars!

The third
Friday in May
is National
Pizza Party Day
in the United
States.

Pizza-flavored snacks

From mini pizzas to pizza-flavored chips to pizza sticks, there were now options for every kind of snacker. And that included dessert—one company even created a pizza-flavored ice cream featuring swirls of tomato jam and mozzarella.

Pizza Pop

By now, it's probably clear that many people around the world like—no, love—pizza. After all, they have adapted it to their own tastes, eaten it at all hours, morphed it into different delicacies, and and even thrown pizza-themed parties. But the world's love of pizza goes beyond just eating it. Pizza has become so popular that it is now a part of pop culture, from fashion to music to media and more.

That's right—pizza isn't just iconic, it's now a fashion icon in its own right. Today, people can sport shirts, pants, dresses, and more covered in images of pizzas or bearing pizza-related slogans. In fact, Pizza Hut even released an official line of clothing! But Domino's was not to be outdone—an Australian location created a diamond-covered pizza-shaped engagement ring worth $9,000. And it wasn't the only one.

Fork or Fingers?

In the United States, most people won't hesitate to grab a slice of piping hot pizza with their hands. But some people prefer to use a knife and fork. This makes a lot of sense in places like Italy, where pizzas are served whole and not in slices. It also works much better for pizzas that are extra messy or super thick, like deep-dish pizzas.

Plenty of jewelry brands sell pizza-themed bling, from watches to necklaces to earrings and more. You can also wear pizza-flavored lip gloss. But if pizza clothing, pizza jewelry, and pizza makeup isn't enough for you, there's more: There are costumes that let you dress up as pizza.

If fashion isn't your thing, fret not. Pizza also appears in music, movies, cartoons, and television. Musical artists like the

Jonas Brothers and the K-pop group Stray Kids have lyrics about pizza in their songs. It just goes to show how much pizza has become a part of the global culture.

And there's even more cheesy goodness on the screen. The Teenage Mutant Ninja Turtles, part of a cartoon television series that began in the 1980s, were famous for their love of pizza . . . and for the strange toppings they ordered. Their pizza orders included peculiar pairings such as chocolate fudge and garlic, marshmallow and pepperoni, and strawberries and anchovy sauce.

Movies from Pixar Animation Studios—such as *Turning Red, Inside Out,* and *Toy Story*—often show a healthy appreciation for pizza. Sometimes they directly dedicate a shot to a pie, or they show the now famous Pizza Planet delivery truck that appears in every single Pixar film made. In fact, after being featured in everything from Marvel movies to cartoons like *Scooby-Doo,* pizza is practically a star.

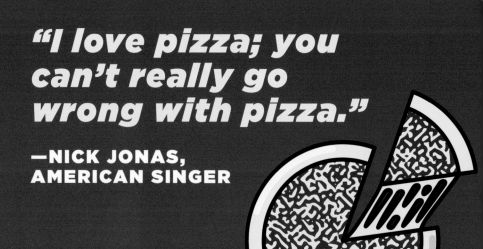

"I love pizza; you can't really go wrong with pizza."
—NICK JONAS, AMERICAN SINGER

In the video game *Fortnite*, characters can don the outfit called Tomatohead to show their devotion to pizza.

Singer Katy Perry snaps a selfie with a fan while dressed in a pizza-themed outfit.

Even celebrities have gotten in on the pizza action over the years. Famous singers and actors—JoJo Siwa, Zendaya, Kumail Nanjiani, Dwayne "The Rock" Johnson—have been snapped digging into slices. Singer Katy Perry has been spotted not only eating pizza, but also tossing slices to her fans—and even wearing a pizza onesie. It's become clear: For many people, pizza is more than a food. It's a way of life!

TOTALLY! PEPPERONI!

Popular Toppings

Pepperoni is the most popular pizza topping in the United States, with sausage coming in as a close second. In Italy, people prefer a classic, Neapolitan-style margherita. But what about the rest of the world? Check out some popular pies around the globe:

- **Going Bananas:** In Sweden, some people top their pizzas with slices of bananas and savory curry powder.
- **Something's Fishy:** Pizza fanatics in Russia opt for *mockba,* a mix of sardines, salmon, mackerel, tuna, and onions.
- **More Mayo:** In Japan, one top choice is *mayo jaga,* a pizza featuring mayonnaise and potatoes.
- **Island Flavor:** People in Costa Rica enjoy topping their pies with shredded coconut.
- **Peas, Please:** Lots of people in Brazil order their slices with this green veggie on top.
- **Cluck, Cluck:** In parts of South Africa, chicken pizzas reign supreme. (However, in other areas, people opt for the classic margherita.)
- **In a Pickle:** Pizzas featuring pickled ginger, mutton, and cheese top the menus in India.
- **Meat Lovers:** Some Australian pizza places create pies topped with kangaroo or alligator meat.
- **I'm Stuffed:** Zanzibar, an island off Tanzania, is home to Zanzibar pizza: a thin, crispy pancake stuffed with ingredients that range from spiced meat to fruit to candy pieces.

A chef in Zanzibar cooks Zanzibar pizza for hungry customers.

In the past decade or so, people have been snacking on more varieties of pizza than ever before. And now, pizza is an option for even more people since many chefs are cooking up recipes with dietary restrictions in mind. Vegans and people with dairy allergies can order pizzas with plant-based cheese made from nuts or soy. People who have gluten allergies also have plenty of options, such as gluten-free crusts made from cauliflower. Today, it seems like pizza does it all. Is it even possible that pizza of the future could be that different?

You bet! When you picture the food of the future, what do you imagine? 3D printed ice cream, liquid meals in a tube, and burgers made by aliens?

Well, we can't guarantee all that stuff, but add pizza to the top of your list. In fact, pizza has been making futuristic history for years. In 2001, Pizza Hut made an incredible pizza delivery . . . to space! Using a rocket, the company sent a pizza straight to the International Space Station (ISS). And in 2022, astronauts aboard the ISS held the first ever pizza party in space, using pizzas they created themselves from a kit.

It's not just space: Pizza is getting futuristic right here on Earth. Companies are creating all kinds of technologically advanced ovens designed to cook pizzas perfectly. Many of these can be installed in kitchens or homes instead of just in restaurants—and some are even portable,

Sustainable Slices

These days, plenty of people are looking for ways to make their foods more sustainable. This means that the food is not farmed or collected in ways that are harmful to people or the planet. One of the most sustainable foods? Insects! While eating insects may seem unusual for people who did not grow up with the practice, it is common in many countries across the world—and becoming more common in others, too. Insects are even starting to appear on pizzas, whether in the dough or as a yummy topping.

Grasshoppers are sometimes used as a pizza topping.

A New Tradition

Naples, Italy, may be the birthplace of traditional Neapolitan pizza, but the city is no stranger to innovation. After World War II, Italian chefs took creativity to new heights when they invented the fried pizza, also called *pizza fritta*. This pizza begins as usual, with a disc of pizza dough topped with cheese and other ingredients. However, the dough is then folded over and sealed, forming a pizza dough semicircle chock-full of toppings. The pizza is then dunked into hot oil, where it fries to a golden brown.

A Domino's
delivery drone

meaning they can be taken from place to place just in case you start craving a slice. Want even more machines? One pizza place in New Jersey sells pizzas created by robots. Other places are keeping things a bit more simple by focusing just on the ingredients—such as using lab-grown meat.

A pizza made
by a 3D printer

What's more, inventors have come up
with machines that don't just cook pizzas
but they print them! That's right, there are
3D printers capable of making pizzas layer
by layer. Normally, 3D printers work by
pouring out superhot liquid plastic that

cools into shapes and objects one layer at a time. With a food 3D printer, the machine combines edible ingredients to make dough, sauce, and cheese, and then pours it out layer by layer. The pizza is then popped in the oven to cook.

And it's not just how pizzas are made that is getting the futuristic treatment; people are also changing how pizzas are ordered and delivered. As technologies continue to change, there are more ways than ever to place a pizza order: from a smartwatch, by asking an artificially intelligent virtual assistant, or even directly from a car. As for how your pizza gets to you, keep your eyes peeled for delivery robots, self-driving cars, and even drones.

From its humble ancient origins, pizza has become a

Pizza vending machines may not be a new idea, but some vending machines can now bake pizzas from scratch, entirely made to order!

part of life around the world. In fact, there truly isn't even one "right" kind of pizza! But one thing is clear: From thick crust to thin, from fast food to homemade gourmet food, and from Earth to space, pizza is here to stay!

Is Pizza Healthy?

While pizza is the ultimate comfort food for many people, is it actually good for your body? On one hand, the cheese on pizza includes calcium, which is important for building strong bones and teeth. Some scientists think lycopene, a chemical found in tomatoes, can help fight diseases. One the other hand, cheese and other toppings like pepperoni are very salty—and eating too much salt can increase the risk of heart problems.

Still, there are ways to make your slice more nutritious. Top your pizza with colorful mixed veggies, which provide vitamins and minerals important for your diet. Homemade pizzas made from scratch tend to be less fatty than frozen or restaurant pizzas. You could also look for crusts made with whole wheat flour which have more fiber and don't change your blood sugar levels as quickly as regular white flour. This also means that you'll avoid the sleepy, sluggish feeling you get after eating a lot of pizza!

The bottom line is that pizza isn't the healthiest meal, but it also depends on what kind you eat . . . and how much of it you eat. Like almost all foods, pizza is best when eaten in moderation!

In a popular
trend on
social media,
people made
"pizza salads,"
salads meant to
taste like pizza,
by adding
popular pizza
toppings.

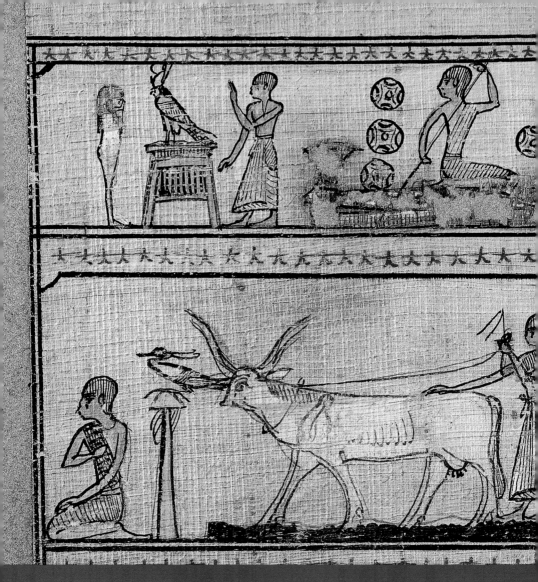

Around 12,000 BCE

Some of the world's first bread is baked in what is now Jordan.

6,000 BCE

Cheese is becoming more common.

1548

Tomatoes arrive in Italy for the first time from the Americas.

An ancient Egyptian illustration showing farmers harvesting wheat

1799

The oldest known cookbook featuring a recipe for tomato sauce is written in Italy.

1889

Queen Margherita of Italy visits Naples, where she is presented with a mozzarella, tomato sauce, and basil pizza. Pizza's popularity skyrockets across the country.

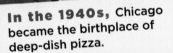

In the 1940s, Chicago became the birthplace of deep-dish pizza.

Late 19th century

Due to hardships, many Italians leave Italy in search of new opportunities. The majority travel to the United States, Argentina, and Brazil.

1905

Lombardi's, one of the first pizza restaurants in the United States, opens in New York City.

1940s

Pizza gains popularity in the United States following World War II.

1943

One of the first restaurants featuring deep-dish pizza opens in Chicago, Illinois.

1946

Detroit-style pizza debuts in Detroit, Michigan.

1950s

The first frozen pizzas are sold.

1958

The first Pizza Hut opens in Kansas.

1959

Little Caesars opens in Michigan.

Workers prepare pizzas on a frozen pizza factory assembly line.

1960

Domino's opens its first location in Michigan.

1962

A Greek immigrant in Canada invents Hawaiian-style pizza.

Astronauts enjoy a pizza party on the International Space Station.

1973

Pizza Hut opens its first location in Japan.

1980s

California-style pizza appears.

1995

Stuffed-crust pizza debuts.

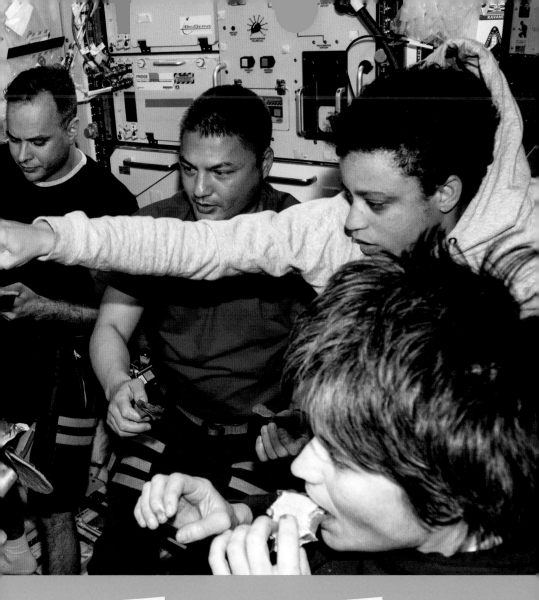

2001

Pizza Hut delivers a pizza to the International Space Station.

2022

The astronauts aboard the ISS have the first pizza party in space.

Build It Yourself!

The savory story of pizza is one that involves creativity, problem-solving, and passion. Get your own innovation bubbling with these activities!

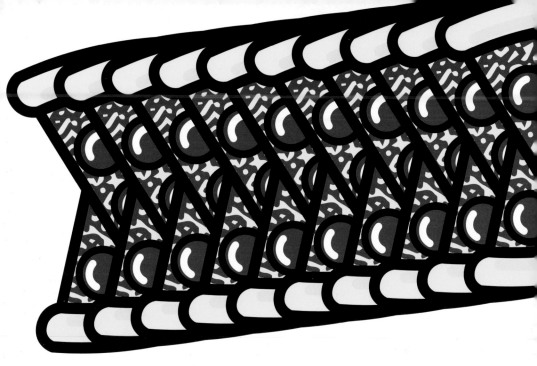

Just Like Pizza

Over the years, people have created lots of new pizzalike dishes and invented new and unusual ways to eat pizza—from pizza-flavored ice cream to handheld pizza pockets. Try dreaming up a new form of pizza. If you're stuck, try thinking about an area where you think pizza could be improved. Is it too messy? Too hot? Then come up with something that could solve this problem, making pizza even better.

Cool Combinations

Today, there are tons of pizza toppings in existence, with even more combinations. Can you dream up something new? Try balancing out flavors to include something salty, something sweet, and something creamy. What was the inspiration for your new pizza? What is it called?

Amazing Art

It's no secret that people truly love pizza. In fact, humans love pizza so much they've created songs about it, wear clothing and jewelry inspired by it, and even dress up as it for Halloween. Explore your artistic side, and come up with a new, creative way to honor pizza. It could be a poem, a new song, or some cool new pizza gear.

Glossary

Curdling: The process of going sour, or separating into liquids and clumps known as curds

Enzyme: A substance that helps start chemical reactions in living organisms

Fermentation: The breaking down of a substance caused by tiny organisms such as bacteria or yeast

Franchise: A business that allows a partner to sell a product or good under the business's name

Globalization: The process of making the world more interconnected through trade, travel, and technology

Glocalization: The changing of a global company's product or marketing to suit local needs and preferences

Import: To bring in a good or service from a foreign country

Nomadic: Moving from place to place without settling or living in one area

Suburb: The outer part of a city or town, usually where many people reside

Yeast: A type of fungus often used in baking to help bread rise or to cause foods and liquids to ferment

Note: Some of these words may have more than one meaning. These definitions match what the words mean in this book.

Index

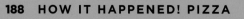